PLAY ON WORDS

R.R. NOALL

DEDICATION

To those who didn't say I was crazy for wanting to be a writer — thank you.

My college essay explored my love affair with words. The way they roll off of my tongue. The way that we, as speakers and writers, control their meaning. This collection of poetry explores the use of idioms. They are phrases we say regularly, however, they are not often understood, investigated, or given a second thought.

In Play On Words, idioms are used as a tool to explore my journey as a writer and human, who for better or worse, finds meaning in everything.

"There is nothing to writing. All you do is sit down at a typewriter and bleed."

Ernest Hemingway

PLAY ON WORDS

Best of Both Worlds

A professional juggling act on a side street.
Passersby gather to see the show.
A circus act, demanding so many eyes.
A trance, beckoning "ah's" and claps.
Wallets open — captivated.
The street rat takes a bow, before returning
Home to the shadows.

Whole Nine Yards

Feet away, really, but more.
It seems farther.
Hoping to cross the line,
Despite the grueling obstacles ahead.
How far would you go to meet me in the middle?

Elvis Has Left the Building

Silent goodbyes, marked by short glances
Across shapes undefined.
Some things don't need words.

A Penny for Your Thoughts

What I would give to take
One
Peek
Inside of your mind.
I see things stirring there,
Silently making ripples in your life.

Will it all implode or will you thrive?

An Arm and a Leg

Pieces chipped away,
Getting larger as time ticks by.
Then suddenly, you see yourself in a mirror and
Have no idea who you are.
No one is worth that much.

At the Drop of a Hat

Throwing it all up in the air, I shrugged.
Juggling got a bit too hard in the dark.
A beautiful sight – everything I never needed,
Turning into a firework for the world to see.

Bite Off More Than You Can Chew

I am hungry for them.
Every piece of you.
Even the things that might leave a sour taste in my
Mouth.
The parts you hide away in the closet.

The question is, will you share them?

Let them spill out and be messy,
Leaving stains in inconvenient places.
I will love them anyway.

Burn the Midnight Oil

The quiet has a sound if you listen hard enough.
Shallow breaths.
A pulse.
The noise sheets make when you move in bed.
The air gives you the shivers,
But the kind you don't try to stop.
They're the kind you crave,
Because feeling the world hit you feels good.
All of these things happen just after midnight,
And I wonder why everyone is
So eager for the sunrise.

Drastic Times, Drastic Measures

Once upon a time, I thought I might be crazy.
No high ledge was going to make it better.
Being on this plane would have to do;
Staying in the lanes of other's rules.

Curiosity Killed the Cat

Maybe you pushed too hard,
Even though I never faltered in your eyes.
Perhaps your thoughts hit me
Like jagged and rusted spears,
Thrown through your teeth.
It's possible that I read too much into your words.
Always something to say,
Never anything worthwhile.

Devil's Advocate

Let me explain just one more time.
Have your way with my words – rearrange and
Twist them.
They'll always be true.
I'm certain of that.

Hit the Nail On the Head

I had your number the second I met you.
The stench of arrogance
Traveled with you into every room,
Between you and everyone you spoke to.
I was right about you, unfortunately.
No one wants to be right about a person like that,
Because no such person should be allowed to exist.

One-Way Ticket

An undeniable decision
The moment I looked into your eyes.
A one-way ticket kind of star-struck —
The type of love you don't come back from.

Put My Thumb On It

You were a reoccurring dream
I couldn't quite remember.
A light in my darkest corners, stirring feelings in
Familiar but distant places.
You were there all along, calling me home.

Method to the Madness

In my head it all made sense.
Words you spoke that cut — I deserved it.
The cold shoulder when I felt alone — meant to
Show me I am strong.
Tears I silently cried — secrets I couldn't share.
It only made sense for so long.

Needle in a Haystack

Kerosene among timbers,
Ready to set it all on fire — you were the spark
I was waiting for.

Achilles' Heel

A weakness I choose — bowing to you
At the end of every day.
My solace.
My altar.
My saving grace.

Wild Goose Chase

Books with small print say that love is hard.
Haphazard.
Unbearable.
Destructive.

Pounding hearts shouldn't come from the chase,
But from the stillness.
The quiet.
A calm found between souls cemented in fate.
Rushing blood, but steady.
Meant to be.

Catch 22

A roundabout of decisions,
None of them right.
It's funny how we're okay with moving in
Stagnant circles.
False productivity, slowing us down.

Once in a Blue Moon

Staring down a glass bottle
Eyes filled by a blue moon.
An extra celestial happening — rare.
Like the way I'd rather not speak
Than slur my words.

A Perfect Storm

You're the rumble to my lightning —
The sound bringing life to my sparks.

Bite the Bullet

The churning in your stomach
Urges you forward.
An apocalyptic premonition without a savior.

Hesitation and adrenaline
Are a deadly combination.

Cold Shoulder

Hollow greetings, even on the sunniest days.
Vacant hearts look a lot like empty wine bottles.
Close your eyes and enjoy a moment of silence.
The quiet before the storm — the typhoon brewing
Between you and yourself.

X Marks the Spot

Treasure hidden away.
Reserved for the outcasts searching for hope.
That's the problem with looking for answers in
Secret places.
Nothing worth having is buried.
Good things lay in plain sight.

Right.
Under.
Your.
Nose.

Cut a Rug

Star-studded eyes, the object of everyone's affection.
No words can describe.
No image able to capture
The way she strode into the room,
Stealing hearts and fanning daydreams.

On the Fence

There's only a line between sober and euphoria.
A momentary decision, from tiptoe to racing,
Made in a single breath.

Turn the Other Cheek

One-sided words won't hurt,
Don't grow a conscience now.
Bruises fade far too quickly for your nonsense.

Grain of Salt

Rough grains,
Bitter sandpaper in my mouth — the reason I lose
My words in my head.
Unable to put together the pieces.
Living in a flashback.

Bent Out of Shape

From 9 to 5, a smile works wonders.
A happy mask you can't bear to shed.
Deep breaths begin at 5:01 — your only
Honest moment.
Each night, you waste away a bit more.
A gradual ruin.
Your insides, that twist all day, are finally able to
Break through your skin.
The monster rears its head, just in time
For you to sleep.

It Takes Two to Tango

Radios communicating via satellite,
Creating a wave so precise — so purposeful.
A call that can't possibly go unanswered.
But it does.

Speak of the Devil

Words spitting venom, toxic.
Eyes blur — the beginning of the end.
A slow-pulse panic attack,
Knowing there's no antidote to save you.

A Piece of Cake

Taking bites in slow motion
Savoring the flavor, each a nuance on my tongue.

Under the Weather

My thoughts were unmanageable.
Quickly, I regretted my raincoat.
I tried to interrupt the rain,
Knowing I'm happier hood down and damp.

Play On Words

Smooth, like the dice in my hand.
Seemingly leaving it all to chance, a careless toss.
Words don't fall on pages like that.
They're graceful.
Calculated.
Yet we play.

ABOUT THE AUTHOR

R.R. Noall is a poet, writer, and creator. An Ohio native now living in Colorado, she spends her days writing professionally and creatively. From a young age, Rachel knew she would be a writer. This love was affirmed for her at Allegheny College, where she studied English literature.

In early 2018, Noall founded From Whispers to Roars, a Denver-based literary and arts magazine. She is also currently pursuing her MA in Creative Writing from the University of Denver.

In her free time, Rachel explores Colorado, drinks hoppy beer, and tries to watch the sunset every evening.

Play On Words is her debut poetry collection. Rachel writes poetry daily on her social media channels. Keep up with her writing pursuits at www.rrnoall.com.

Follow R.R. Noall on social media:

Instagram: @rrnoall

Twitter: @rrnoall

Facebook: @rrnoall